ASMR
Coloring Book

50 tingly triggers

Relaxation & Tingles | Over 250 ASMR Artist Featured

ALIEN

Who would've guessed that alien abduction would be such a trigger for so many people. ASMR is a strange thing. But for many, the hypnotic quality of being examined by an alien entity can be an incredibly pleasurable experience.

ARTIST CREATING UNIQUE VIDEOS TO THIS TRIGGER

Ephemeral Rift

Ruby True ASMR

FrivolousFox ASMR

Nebula ASMR

ASMR Shanny

DreamMaker ASMR

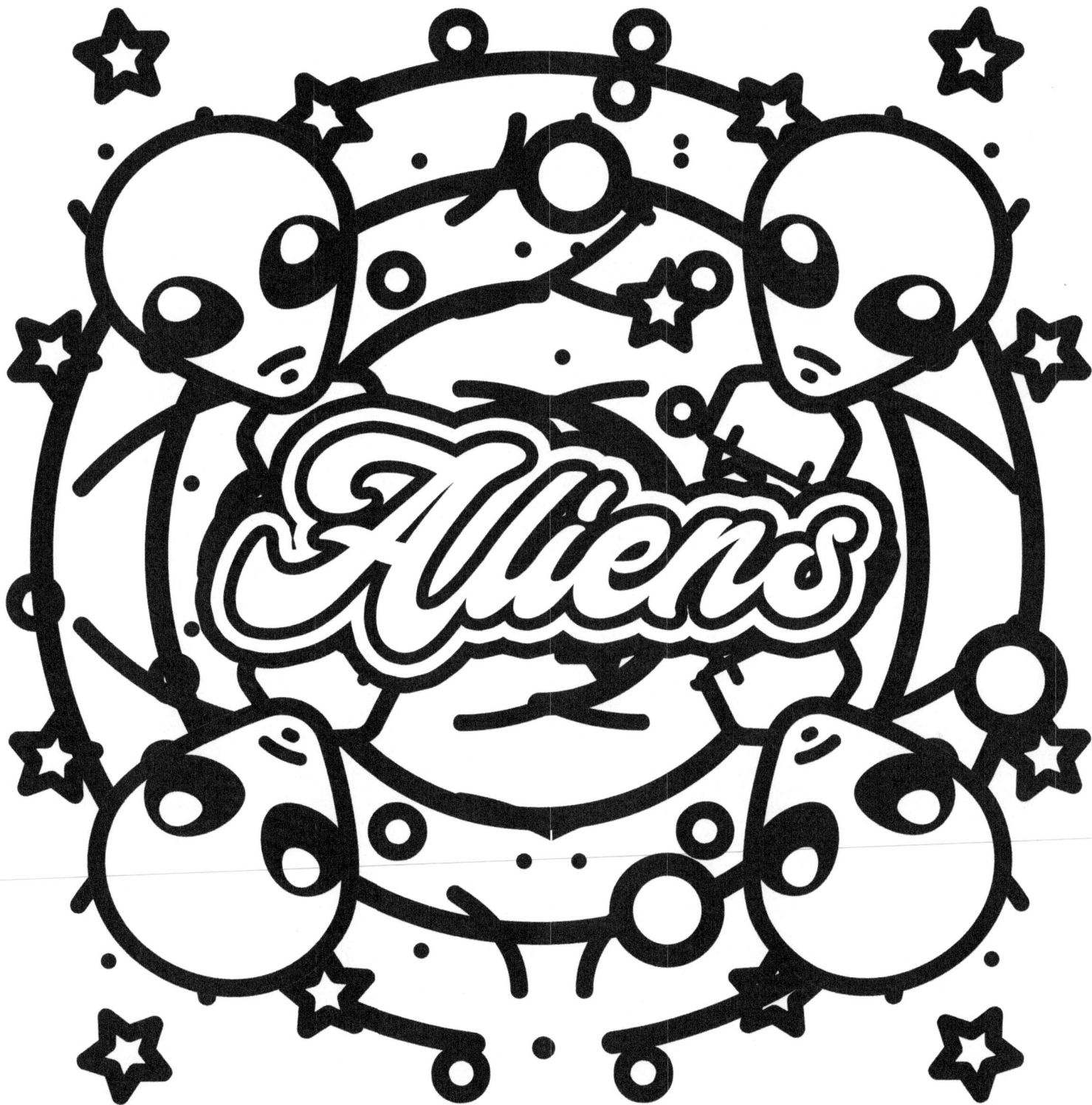

BACK SCRATCHING

Whether you're a tingle-head or not, most people find back-scratching a delightful experience. A similar joy comes from just watching backs getting scratched. Maybe it's those mirror neurons triggering that create the magic. Who knows?

ARTIST CREATING UNIQUE VIDEOS TO THIS TRIGGER

emvy ASMR

DOOBOO ASMR

Avalon In Wonderland

ASMR -T

Haus of ASMR

RelaxWithReena

search artist + "trigger"

BEDTIME

Bedtime is such a special time. As a child, it was a time of relaxation and comfort. Many of us had books read to us by our parents. If only bedtime was this easy as an adult. Most bedtime videos try to capture that same calm, cozy experience.

ARTIST CREATING UNIQUE VIDEOS TO THIS TRIGGER

fallenshadow asmr	PJ Dreams ASMR
Madi ASMR	Prim ASMR
SophieMichelle ASMR	Rosy ASMR

search artist + "trigger"

BRUSHING

Brushing comes in many forms, but anyway you imagine it, it's a comforting experience. And highly sensory! Imagine that brush along your scalp, that swishing sound passing along your ear. For many, brushing triggers a very tingly experience.

ARTIST CREATING UNIQUE VIDEOS TO THIS TRIGGER

Alana ASMR	ASMR Love by T&P
ASMR saloon and massage	ASMR Bakery
RaffyTaphyASMR	CrinkleLuvin ASMR

search artist + "trigger"

COOKIES

So many ASMR triggers harken back to our childhoods. And who can't remember the joy of fresh cookies and milk? This trigger typically involves chewing sounds and comforting roleplays to bring on the goose pimples.

ARTIST CREATING UNIQUE VIDEOS TO THIS TRIGGER

Karuna Satori ASMR

FemaleASMR

Rebecca's Beautiful ASMR Addiction

Ephemeral Rift

SouthernASMR Sounds

Hungry Herbivore ASMR

search artist + "trigger"

DONUTS

Many of us love the sounds of chewing. But there are so many things to chew on! A popular one for ASMR artists is the donut. It works because there are so many donuts, and the sound is a gooey, chewy sonic pleasure.

ARTIST CREATING UNIQUE VIDEOS TO THIS TRIGGER

ASMR MAG UK	Safira Crespin
Mellawnie ASMR	Binaural Eats ASMR
N.E Let's Eat	Sufficient Whispers

search artist + "trigger"

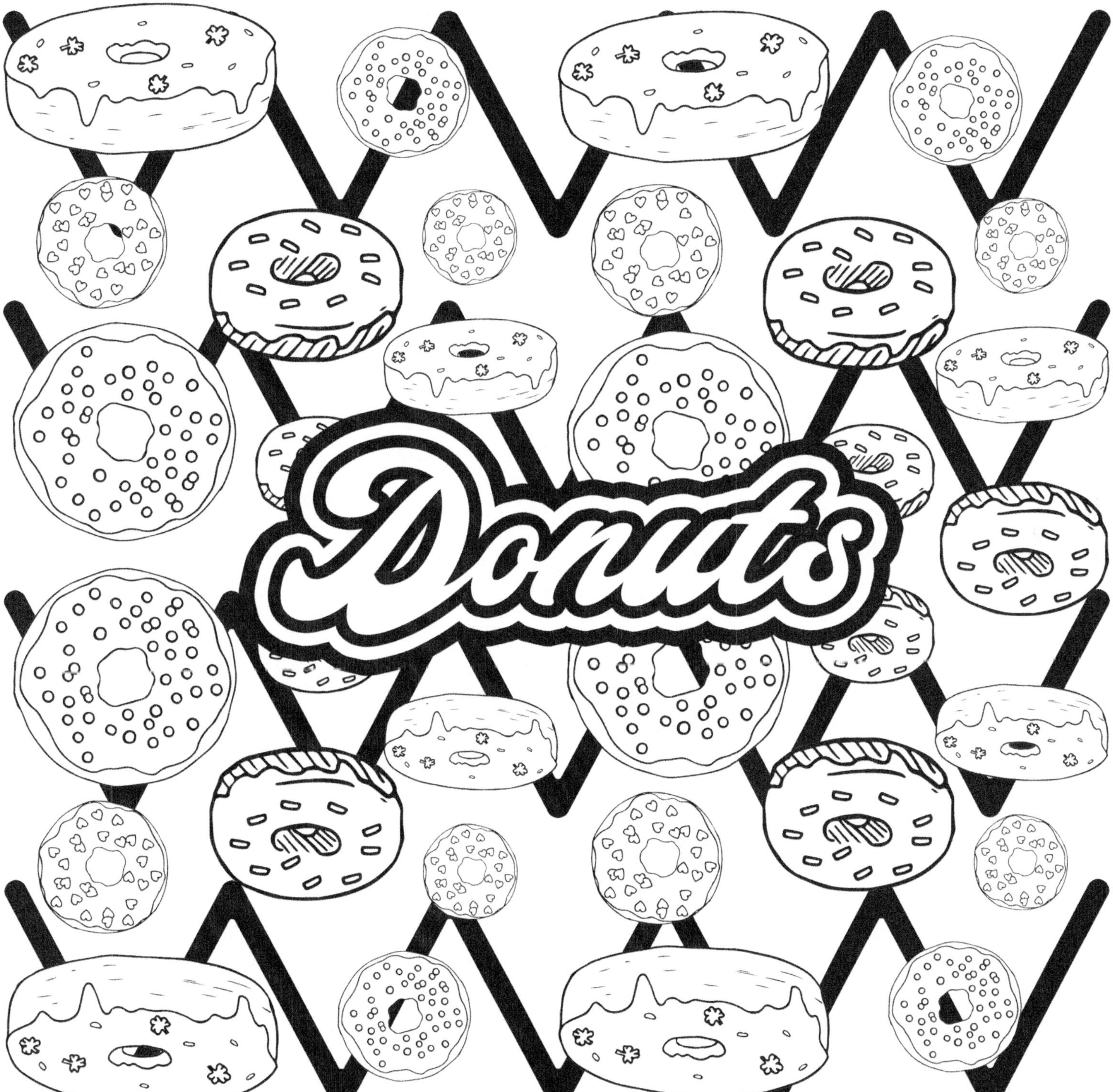
Donuts

EAR CLEANING

The key to ear cleaning triggers is the experience of intense sounds right up close. The faintest sound up along the ear creates incredible tingles. Pair that with an attentive roleplay actor, and you have a really tinglastic tingle fest.

ARTIST CREATING UNIQUE VIDEOS TO THIS TRIGGER

LatreceASMR	Tingting ASMR
DennisASMR	BehindTheMoons
Lizi ASMR	ASMR Bakery

EYE EXAM

One of the classic ropeplays of ASMR. The eye exam features triggers like the attentive examiner performing tasks up close. Often times they will whisper the procedure as they go about. It creates a chilling, wonderful experience.

ARTIST CREATING UNIQUE VIDEOS TO THIS TRIGGER

OZONE ASMR

Articulate Design ASMR

Marno ASMR

Creative Calm ASMR

DiamondASMR

asmr zeitgeist

search artist + "trigger"

FIRE

This may be the ubertrigger. The trigger that existed even before ASMR existed. There's something about watching a campfire crackle that is so relaxing. Luckily, ASMR artists have expanded on this trigger in so many tingly ways.

ARTIST CREATING UNIQUE VIDEOS TO THIS TRIGGER

Nameless Nomad ASMR	VisualSounds1 ASMR
Jim ち ASMR	Ephemeral Rift
ASMR Shanny	Madi ASMR

GAMER

The gamer theme trigger is a grab bag of videos. Some of the more popular videos are handling game controllers or watching game-play. But there's also the game store roleplay and reviews of game collections. Take a look.

ARTIST CREATING UNIQUE VIDEOS TO THIS TRIGGER

Captain ASMR

The ASMR Gamer

Jojo's ASMR

ASMR Gaming News

LotsOfBunnies

Scottish Murmurs ASMR

search artist + "trigger"

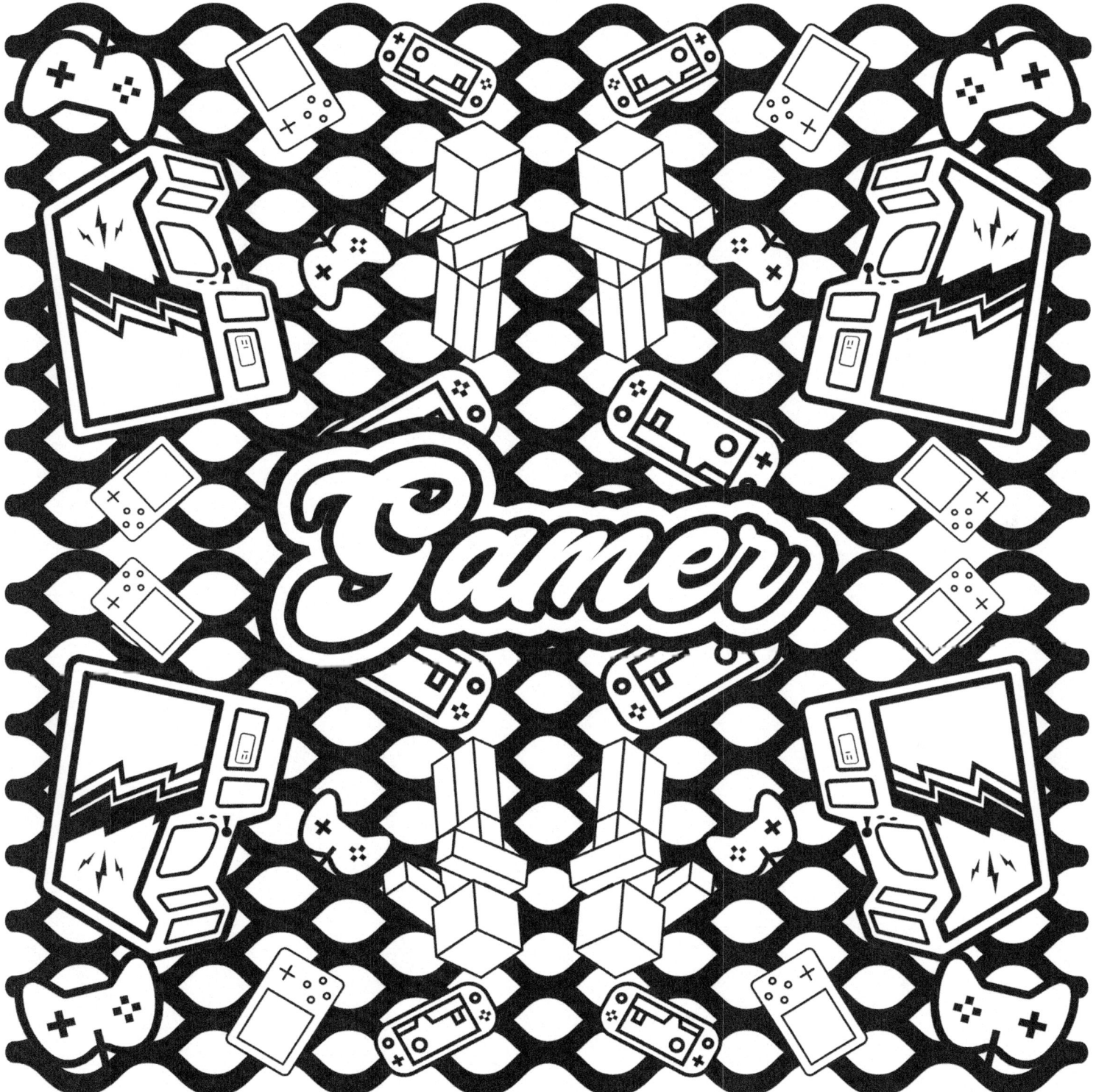

GUM CHEWING

It's not for everyone but for many mouth sounds are a wealth of tingles. And gum chewing accomplishes that better than almost anything else. That juicy, chewing sound of lips smacking bring some tingleheads to heaven.

ARTIST CREATING UNIQUE VIDEOS TO THIS TRIGGER

Mia ASMR

FrivolousFox ASMR

Hannah Confetti

ASMR Leidy

CDub ASMR

Sufficient Whispers

search artist + "trigger"

Gum Chewing

HAIR PLAY

A typical hair play video has at least two people on camera. That alone raises the potential for tingles since you're both listening and watching the hair being played while at the same time seeing the effect on the subject at hand. So Cool.

ARTIST CREATING UNIQUE VIDEOS TO THIS TRIGGER

VisualSounds1 ASMR

Little Me Carmie

ASMR Sharm

ASMR Psychetruth

Goodnight Moon

emvy ASMR

Hair Play

HAIR CUT

The hair cut ASMR video is a smorgasbord of sounds. The splashing of hair being washed. The brushing of hair being combed. The snipping of hair being cut. So many sounds. So many chances for tingles to appear.

ARTIST CREATING UNIQUE VIDEOS TO THIS TRIGGER

Slikhaar TV - Mens hair

[ASMR]nara_

Jazzy ASMR

KevinASMR

Sara Manganese ASMR

Jocie B ASMR

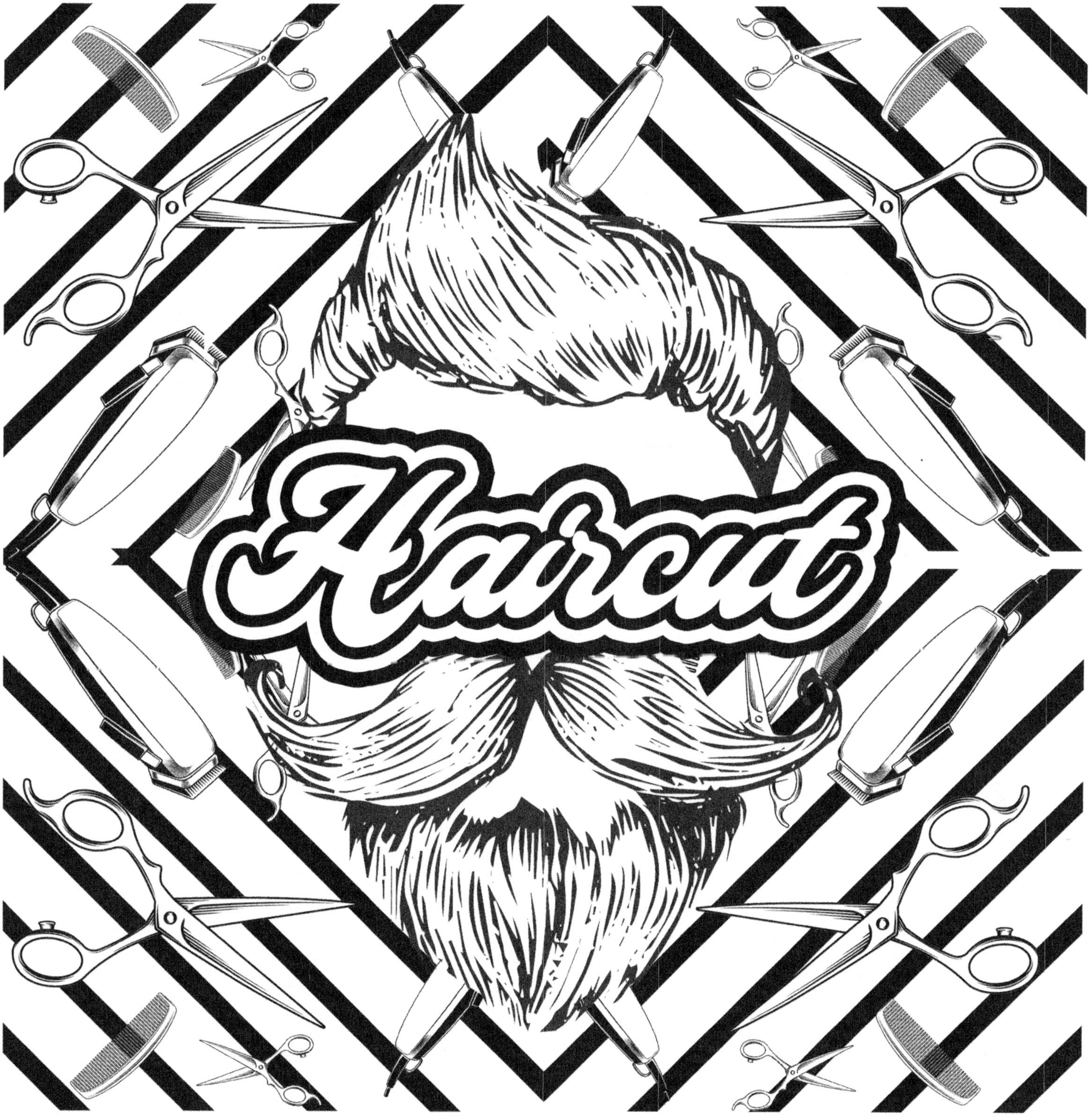
Haircut

HEAD MASSAGE

Imagine soft gentle rubbing of your scalp. Calm stroking along your face and hair. Sweet whispers near your ear. Head massage videos are truly a relaxing experience, and for many a bristle of head tingles. Enjoy!

ARTIST CREATING UNIQUE VIDEOS TO THIS TRIGGER

Chynaunique ASMR

Tena ASMR

Heather Feather ASMR

Angelica

ASMR Suna

ASMR MASSAGE

Head Massage

HONEYCOMB

The crunchy, gooey experience of honeycombs is like nothing else. Among the many foods that trigger tingles, this one is unique in the way it both crunches and oozes. Both a feast for the ears and the eyes.

ARTIST CREATING UNIQUE VIDEOS TO THIS TRIGGER

HunniBee ASMR

立星 LiXing ASMR

FrivolousFox ASMR

Christina ASMR

ZOEY ASMR

freckles asmr

search artist + "trigger"

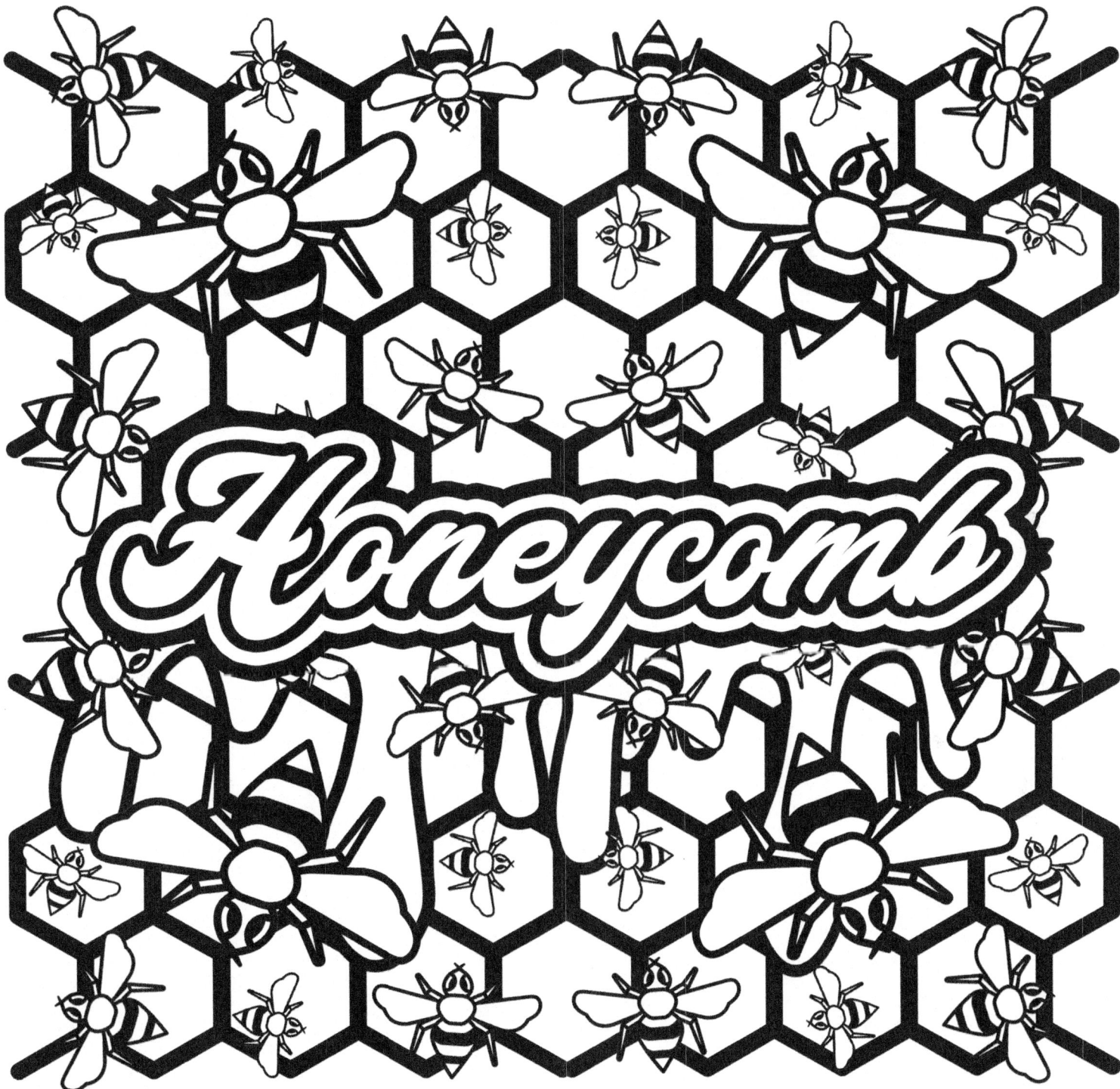

HYPNOSIS

If the spellbinding effect of hypnosis is something you joy, then these videos can turn your tingles into a trancelike state. Both meditative and relaxing these videos are usually more rolepay than actual hypnosis session but the tingle effect is the same.

ARTIST CREATING UNIQUE VIDEOS TO THIS TRIGGER

The ASMR Psychologist

Abby ASMR

Hollow_ VA

ASMR Kay

Karlie Flowz ASMR

ediyasmr

search artist + "trigger"

ICE EATING

Ice has a wide range of sounds. There is the initial crunch of biting into ice, but soon after it turns into a soft slushy sound. It's a delight for tingle-heads who favor mouth sounds, especially those who enjoy the crunchy end of the spectrum.

ARTIST CREATING UNIQUE VIDEOS TO THIS TRIGGER

choa asmr

MINEE EATS

The Thrill ASMR

Ice bites Asmr ooofff

Frozen Asmr

Pastel Ice Eating ASMR

search artist + "trigger"

KEYBOARD

The clickety-clack of keyboard typing is a perfect ASMR trigger. Sometime it's part of a roleplay performance and other times it's simply up-close shots of a proficient typist at work. It's simple but a highly tingly experience.

ARTIST CREATING UNIQUE VIDEOS TO THIS TRIGGER

:3ildcat

filled types

Library of Whispers ASMR

Nicole Ciravolo

Hipyo Tech

MyraASMR

search artist + "trigger"

LATEX GLOVES

For many the fluttering of fingers triggers tingles. Now imagine that paired with the crinkley, rubbery sound of latex. It's a match made in heaven and a delightful experience. Many times these videos also have an element of clinical roleplay.

ARTIST CREATING UNIQUE VIDEOS TO THIS TRIGGER

WhisperSoft

Adorable ASMR

Kindness ASMR

bluezzz ASMR

emi ASMR

KirstDs ASMR

search artist + "trigger"

LIP GLOSS

You'll find that the mouth plays a big role in ASMR. It's at the center for many triggers. But where other mouth triggers focus on the sounds the mouth makes, lip gloss videos also highlight the beauty and mesmerizing effect of the lips alone.

ARTIST CREATING UNIQUE VIDEOS TO THIS TRIGGER

BehindTheMoons

Maddie Leigh ASMR

Marilu Asmr

ASMRslay

Chimikki ASMR

TheCaramel

search artist + "trigger"

LIP SMACKING

This trigger is back to basic. One of the early triggers that became popular, lip smacking produces tingles with its soft, up-close wetted lips. It offers the same tacky, gummy effect that gum chewing produces. A favorite for many.

ARTIST CREATING UNIQUE VIDEOS TO THIS TRIGGER

Nomie Loves ASMR

Jessica ASMR

KevinASMR

AliSerene

ASMR Chi Chi

edafoxx ASMR

search artist + "trigger"

ASMR TRIGGER

MACHINE

The rhythmic whirring and ticking has a hypnotic spell for many ASMRers. But that's just one version of the the endless mechanical sounds that this trigger offers. And the best artist seek out the whole range of this trigger. Have a look for yourself.

ARTIST CREATING UNIQUE VIDEOS TO THIS TRIGGER

Dr. T ASMR

KAYsmr

Miniyu ASMR

Neter Gold - ASMR

Retro White Noise

Gojzer

search artist + "trigger"

MAGIC

You'll find that ASMRers love watching anyone doing anything skillfully. Watching a magician employing their slight of hand falls into that category. And a little soft whisper and now you have the potential for some magical tingles.

ARTIST CREATING UNIQUE VIDEOS TO THIS TRIGGER

Jojo's ASMR

Dido ASMR

SkepticalPickle ASMR

The Lord of ASMR

asmr4u

ASMR Weekly

MAKE-UP

There's a real art to make-up application. And the same way that Bob Ross could pull you in, watching someone skillfully apply make-up can produce massive tingles. Every stroke, every brush can produce goose pimples along your spine!

ARTIST CREATING UNIQUE VIDEOS TO THIS TRIGGER

Gracev	Tingting ASMR
ALB in whisperland ASMR	Peace and Saraity ASMR
Jocie B ASMR	Annura's ASMR

Makeup

MERMAID

Roleplay is an odd development in ASMR. Who know why it took hold? But it's here to stay. And the range of possibilites are as wide as your imagination. It's no wonder then that the mythic mermaid enchants so many ASMRers!

ARTIST CREATING UNIQUE VIDEOS TO THIS TRIGGER

Gibi ASMR

Wanaria ASMR

ASMR da Maru

Oopsydaisy ASMR

Marie-Cécile ASMR

SnowWolf Audio & ASMR

search artist + "trigger"

Mermaids

NAIL TAPPING

Tap tap, tick, tick oh what a relief it is! Or something like that. Nail tapping is a classic of the ASMR community. The mix of beautifully polished nails and that enchanting tapping brings on intense triggers for many. And there's a wide range!

ARTIST CREATING UNIQUE VIDEOS TO THIS TRIGGER

ASMR nails Vera

Triniti J ASMR

stolentoilet ASMR

Queen of Tapping ASMR

Tapping Whispers ASMR

ASMR In Wonderland

Nail Tapping

NATURE

The range of sounds from the great outdoors is as varied as the world. And it's rare to find anyone who doesn't find the sounds of nature to be a relaxing experience. Now bump it up with a fine tingle and you've really got something!

ARTIST CREATING UNIQUE VIDEOS TO THIS TRIGGER

easyASMR

Healing Nature & Meditation

Miss Chloe ASMR

ASMattR ASMR

Anna ASMR

Ephemeral Rift

search artist + "trigger"

NOODLES

This falls into the eating category. And as with all eating sounds, it has its own particular sounds. That soft, squishy, slurpy sound may not be for everyone but for those who fall under its spell--it's magic. It also appeals to the eyes!

ARTIST CREATING UNIQUE VIDEOS TO THIS TRIGGER

Zach Choi ASMR

Binaural Eats ASMR

SAS-ASMR

Chrispy ASMR

ZOEY ASMR

Googly ASMR

search artist + "trigger"

ORIGAMI

Origami is the Japanese tradition of paper folding. Paper folding as art form. And like most skills on display, it has major trigger factors. Watching someone methodically fold and refold while whispering sends shivers throughout your body.

ARTIST CREATING UNIQUE VIDEOS TO THIS TRIGGER

Made In France ASMR	Serenity Seeker ASMR
Gentle Whispering ASMR	GRACE ASMR
rappeler	MrHeadTingles ASMR

search artist + "trigger"

PAINTING

The OG of ASMR triggers thanks to godfather of ASMR, Bob Ross. Many of us fell under its spell gazing at those brush strokes coming across the canvas over and over again. Tiny trees. Peaceful lakes. Big blues skies appearing from nowhere.

ARTIST CREATING UNIQUE VIDEOS TO THIS TRIGGER

Bob Ross

Vadym ShchukinASMR

Isabel imagination ASMR

Nathalie ASMR

Anordaetie

Anne Whisper

search artist + "trigger"

PICKLE EATING

Can you hear that first crunch of biting into a pickle? Nothing sounds quite like it. Its unique blend of crunch and squish is candy to the ear for so many. And it doesn't end there. Every bite has a crunchy goodness.

ARTIST CREATING UNIQUE VIDEOS TO THIS TRIGGER

ASMRTheChew

ASMR LillyVinnily

SECRET SERENITY ASMR

Crunchy ASMR

Rose ASMR

Abbey ASMR

search artist + "trigger"

POKE BOWL

Poke is diced raw fish served either as an appetizer or as a main course. It commonly includes a mixed of vegetables offering the ear a blend of crunchy greens and spongy fish sounds. It's a surprising delight for many ASMRers.

ARTIST CREATING UNIQUE VIDEOS TO THIS TRIGGER

Naomi Eats ASMR

CURIE. ASMR

Kitone ASMR

Nissi ASMR

FAIRY ASMR

PandaEats ASMR

RAIN

Who doesn't enjoy the soothing sounds of rain? This can be an absolute feast for tingle heads! With a blend of soft tapping and low-level buzz, this trigger is known to produce some of the most intesnse tingles across the ASMR triggerdom.

ARTIST CREATING UNIQUE VIDEOS TO THIS TRIGGER

ASMRMagic

Relax Sleep ASMR

SleepDroid Studios

Goodnight Moon

MassageASMR

asmr zeitgeist

search artist + "trigger"

READING

The pleasure of being read to harkens back to our childhood. Especially when the reading is whispered in a soft endearing voice. There are plenty of ASMR artists employing this lovely trigger to shower you with a plethora of tingles.

ARTIST CREATING UNIQUE VIDEOS TO THIS TRIGGER

ATMOSPHERE

Moonlight Cottage ASMR

ediyasmr

PJ Dreams ASMR

Jingle Jangle ASMR

ASMR Sharm

search artist + "trigger"

Reading

REIKI

Reiki is a healing technique that aims to channel energy in a person employing touch to assist in the body's natural healing processes and develop emotional, mental, and spiritual well-being. This super relaxing experience brings on tingles too!

ARTIST CREATING UNIQUE VIDEOS TO THIS TRIGGER

Silver Hare

Reiki with Anna

The Lune INNATE

LottieLoves ASMR

Reiki Healing Hope ASMR

PARIS ASMR

search artist + "trigger"

SHAVING

The focus is usually on men, but anyone can enjoy this old school skill and the tingles it brings on. If you're a fan of watching someone do something well, then you'll love this category of triggers. Watch some experts do their thing.

ARTIST CREATING UNIQUE VIDEOS TO THIS TRIGGER

HairCut Harry

ASMR Glow

Holly Rosi

Celaine's ASMR

ObviouslyASMR

Myaling ASMR

Shaving

SHOES

Shoes are a favorite trigger. Displaying a collection of shoes can be incredibly relaxing. It may be connected to that first shoe-trying experience at the mall. Whatever the case, the many textures and visuals of shoes make this a great trigger.

ARTIST CREATING UNIQUE VIDEOS TO THIS TRIGGER

Jason Dornstar

Matty Tingles

Isabel imagination ASMR

Shoes

SKETCHING

Is there anything better than the scratch scratch scratch of pencil against paper? Add to that, the hypnotic quality of watching a piece of art come to life stroke by stroke. It makes sketching a highly tingle-inducing trigger!

ARTIST CREATING UNIQUE VIDEOS TO THIS TRIGGER

Late Night Tingles ASMR

Amy Kay ASMR

PierreG ASMR

Rinspirit_art

Scottish Undertones

aussieASMRguy

search artist + "trigger"

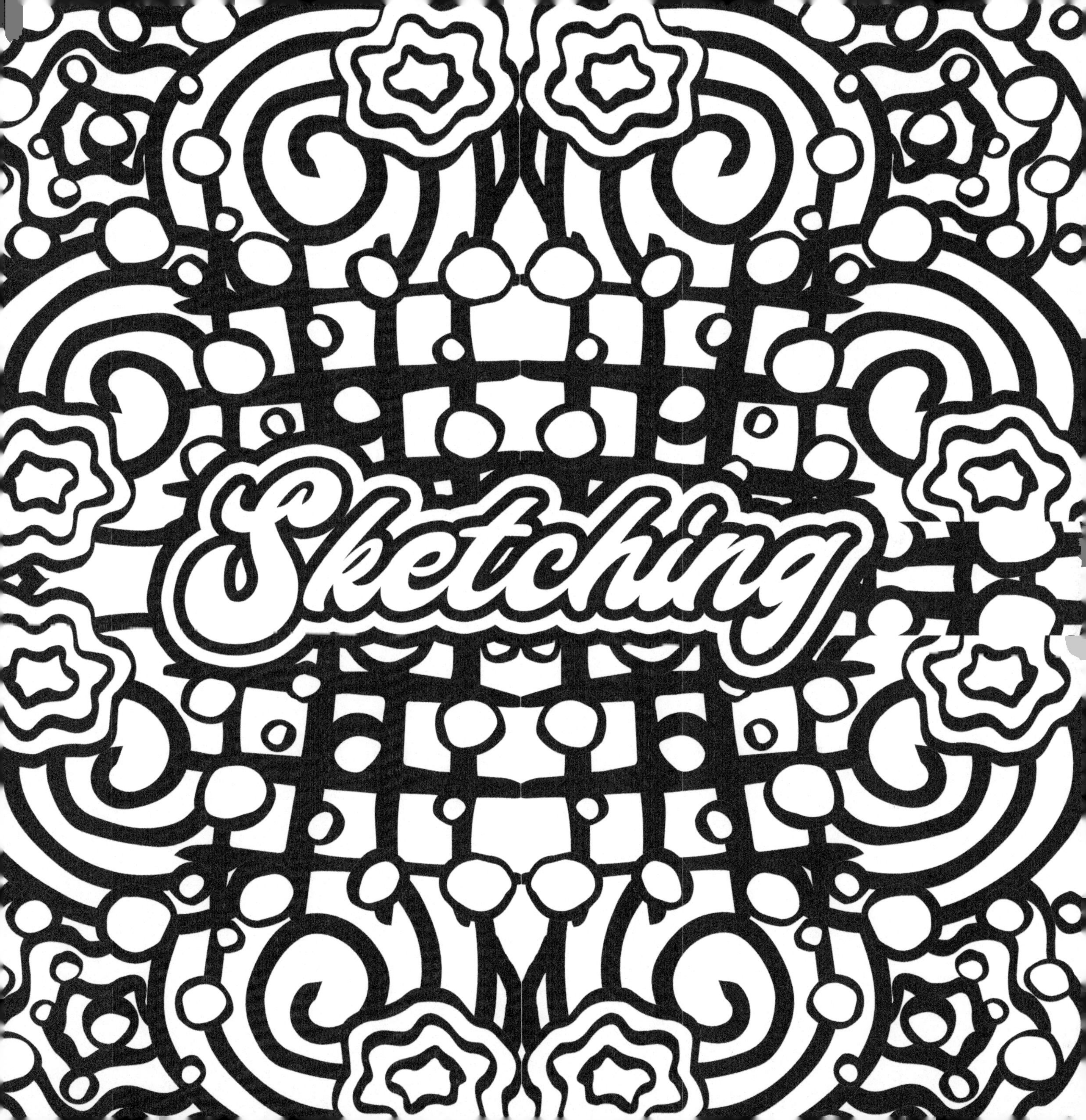
Sketching

SLEEP CLINIC

ASMR was born from the want to relax and have a better night's sleep. It's no surprise then that the sleep clinic roleplay is so popular. That wonderful feeling of quiet attention. The whole experience revolves around the relaxation and tingles.

ARTIST CREATING UNIQUE VIDEOS TO THIS TRIGGER

asmr zeitgeist

Made In France ASMR

Karuna Satori ASMR

Nymfy Official

The ASMR Psychologist

James Matthew ASMR

search artist + "trigger"

Sleep Clinic

SLIME

If you're unfamiliar with the slime niche, you're in for a treat. It's one of the most popular categories and whole channels are dedicated to this one trigger. One video in and you'll see how slime is a spectacle to the senses!

ARTIST CREATING UNIQUE VIDEOS TO THIS TRIGGER

The Best Satisfying	Slime ASMR Videos
StacyAster	Talisa Tossell
Jenny's ASMR	Isabella C ASMR

SUSHI

Ready for some intense eating sounds? Many of the ASMR artist who focus on sushi eating as a trigger use fantastic equipment to really capture the sounds of that squishy, cruchy delight. Sushi may not be for everyone but try it as a triggger.

ARTIST CREATING UNIQUE VIDEOS TO THIS TRIGGER

N.E ASMR	eatingwdaniel
SAS-ASMR	SongByrd ASMR
Fume	DennisASMR

search artist + "trigger"

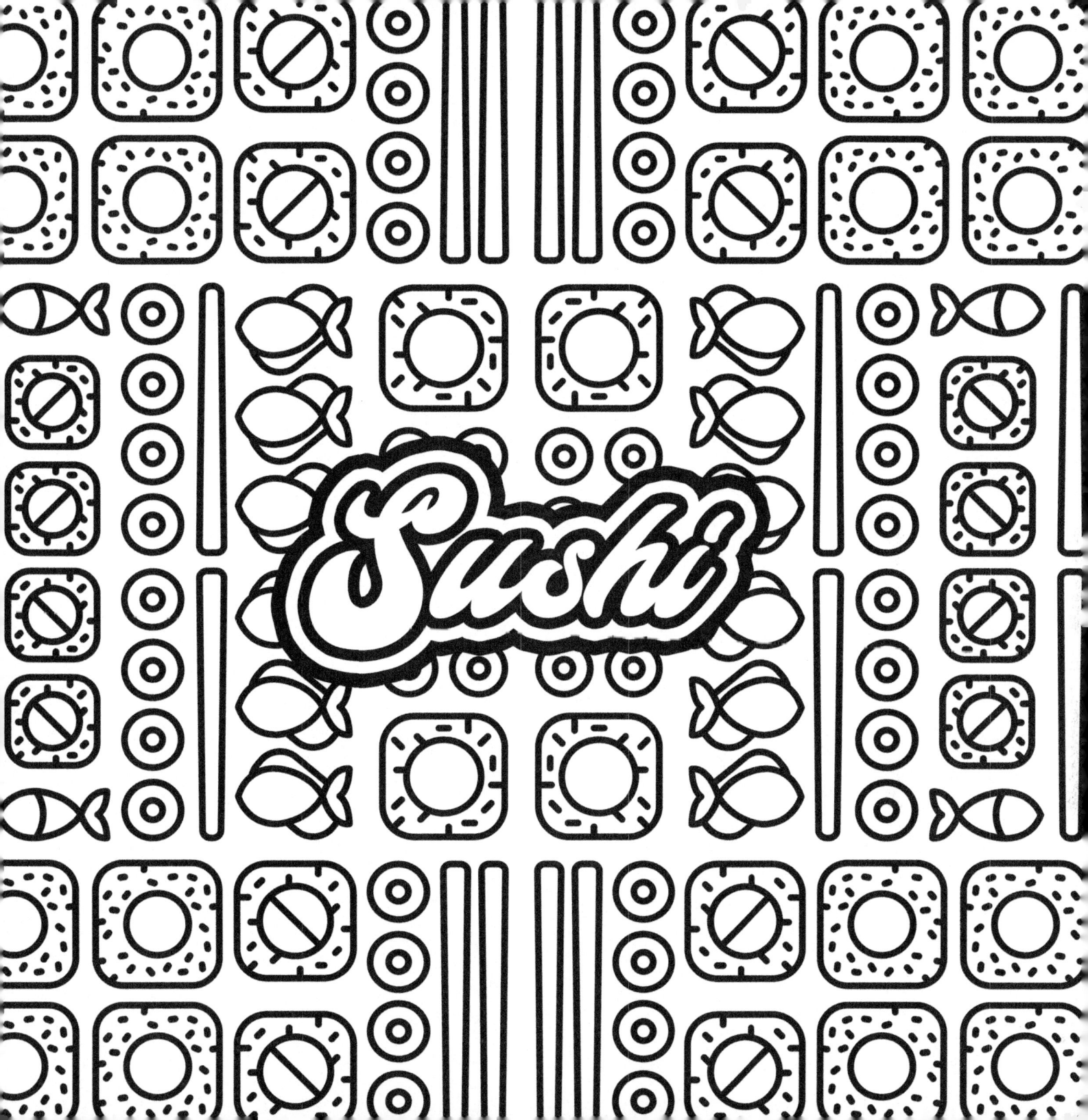

TEA

Tea is relaxing. Tea drinking and tea making both trigger big tingles. Even if you're not a big tea drinker you can enjoy the lovely experience of watch tea be carefully brewed and poured. There's a whole array of sounds that you'll enjoy.

ARTIST CREATING UNIQUE VIDEOS TO THIS TRIGGER

Goodnight Moon

Myaling ASMR

WhispersRed ASMR

ASMR twodae

ASMR MASSAGE FUN

theASMRnerd

TRIGGER WORDS

This has taken years to develop but did you know there are a list of words that induce the greatest level of tingles! Yup, and ASMR artist have been hard at work finding and listing trigger words that produce the biggest tingles imaginable.

ARTIST CREATING UNIQUE VIDEOS TO THIS TRIGGER

Tena ASMR

Slight Sounds ASMR

The ASMR Ryan

Lin ASMR

Fabled Fawn ASMR

ASMR Lia

Trigger Words

TUNING FORKS

There's a way in which the tone of a tuning fork can vibrate with what feels like the vibrations of your soul. It flows through you. Buzzes your head and rains tingles all over your body. It's a magnificient experience for fans of ASMR.

ARTIST CREATING UNIQUE VIDEOS TO THIS TRIGGER

FredsVoice ASMR	Ephemeral Rift
Yew Berry ASMR	The Lune INNATE
ZhiMaasmr	ASMR by Becky

search artist + "trigger"

UNBOXING

Those outside of the ASMR world may find it surprising that unboxing can trigger such an enjoyable experience. But it's hard to resist that swish sound of a hand on carboard, the crinkle of unpackaged plastic and the surprises awaiting us.

ARTIST CREATING UNIQUE VIDEOS TO THIS TRIGGER

Morpheus ASMR

WhisperAudios ASMR

kota asmr

RVasmr

Slimeowy

ALEX's Miniature Cooking

search artist + "trigger"

ASMR TRIGGER

WATERMELON

Watermelon works on many levels. First there is the blend of crunchy and juicy sounds coming at you. Followed by the mushy gulp. Plus you have the bright pinks and greens radiating from the screen. Added together it equals a sweet tingle party.

ARTIST CREATING UNIQUE VIDEOS TO THIS TRIGGER

suellASMR

ASMR With Oscar

ASMR GRANDPA

Animal ASMR

Gril ASMR

Bites Only ASMR

search artist + "trigger"

WHISPERING

Some may argue that whispering is the heart and soul of ASMR. The first few online videos created centered on the soothing sensation of someone whispering sweet, attentive words. To this day, whispering is sought after for its tingle potency.

ARTIST CREATING UNIQUE VIDEOS TO THIS TRIGGER

Gentle Whispering ASMR

FrivolousFox ASMR

Zach Choi ASMR

ASMR PPOMO

Gibi ASMR

mads asmr

search artist + "trigger"

WOOD CARVING

Wood carving taps into an assortment of sound. Wood chips, scratches, crunches, snaps and buckles. And watching a project slowly take form from a block of wood is hypnotic. It taps into that other obsession of ASMR fans: artistry.

ARTIST CREATING UNIQUE VIDEOS TO THIS TRIGGER

ASMRSurge

ASMR Dream More

ASMR Ouvir

Lucia Ferri

ASMR RandomSpace

Alexander Grabovetskiy

search artist + "trigger"

WOOD TAPPING

There's all sorts of tapping in the ASMR community and part of the charm is discovering unusual sensations from unusual object. But wood tapping holds a place of its own. It's capable of producing both a light and deep thud sound. Tingle, tingle!

ARTIST CREATING UNIQUE VIDEOS TO THIS TRIGGER

Vito ASMR

Queen of Tapping ASMR

SCREW ASMR

ASMR Sinabro

JayLynn ASMR

Coromo Sara. ASMR

ZEN GARDEN

The Zen garden seems a perfect fit to the ASMR community. As if this ancient tradition inspired the movement itself. It's both relaxing and stimulating. A great Zen video is capable of producing an assortment of visuals and sounds to relax you.

ARTIST CREATING UNIQUE VIDEOS TO THIS TRIGGER

ASMRSurge

ASMRplanet

Made In France ASMR

ASMR Love by T

KT 65

ASMR Destiny

Printed in Great Britain
by Amazon